ALLOSAURUS

by Janet Riehecky
illustrated by Llyn Hunter

Created by

Distributed by CHILDRENS PRESS ®
Chicago, Illinois

*Grateful appreciation is expressed to Bret S. Beall,
Curatorial Coordinator for the Department of Geology,
Field Museum of Natural History, Chicago, Illinois,
who reviewed this book to insure its accuracy.*

CHILDRENS PRESS HARDCOVER EDITION
ISBN 0-516-06276-X

CHILDRENS PRESS PAPERBACK EDITION
ISBN 0-516-46276-8

Library of Congress Cataloging in Publication Data

Riehecky, Janet, 1953-
  Allosaurus / by Janet Riehecky ; illustrated by Llyn Hunter.
  p. cm. — (Dinosaurs)
  Summary: Introduces the physical characteristics, habits, and
natural environment of the huge dinosaur whose name means "different
lizard."
  ISBN 0-89565-421-0
  1. Allosaurus—Juvenile literature. [1. Allosaurus.
2. Dinosaurs.] I. Hunter, Llyn, ill. II. Title. III. Series:
Riehecky, Janet, 1953-   Dinosaurs.
QE862.S3R52   1988
567.9'7—dc19   88-1693
                                  CIP
                                    AC

1 2 3 4 5 6 7 8 9 10 11 12 R 97 96 95 94 93 92 91 90 89

ALLOSAURUS

Many years ago the earth was ruled by
strange creatures called dinosaurs.

The name dinosaur means "terrible
lizard." But dinosaurs weren't really
lizards, and not all of them were terrible.

Some were as large as your house.

Others were as small as your dog.

Some were plant eaters.

Some were meat eaters.

One type of dinosaur was called the
Allosaurus (al-uh-SAWR-us), which means
"other lizard." The Allosaurus was a huge
dinosaur—as big as a bus! It stood six-
teen feet high, was thirty-five feet long,
and weighed as much as a small truck.

It had a big, grinning mouth—but other dinosaurs learned not to trust that smile. It hid sharp teeth that were three inches long!

The Allosaurus was a hunter, and it used its big, sharp teeth to eat other animals. Sometimes a hungry Allosaurus would bite into an animal so hard, it would break some of its teeth. But it didn't have to worry about that. New teeth grew in whenever any teeth came out.

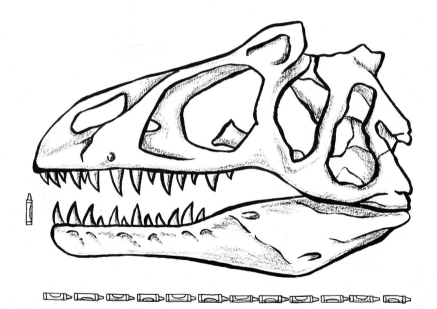

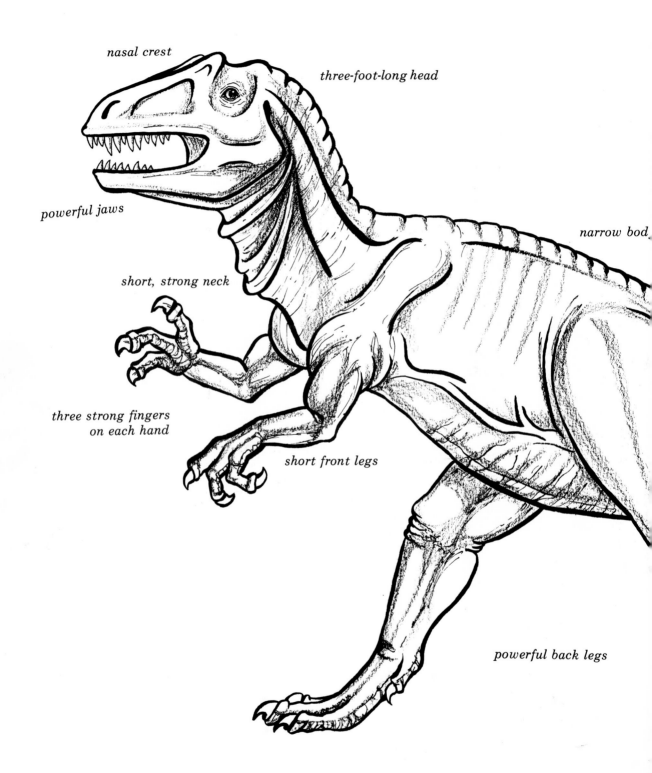

nasal crest

three-foot-long head

powerful jaws

narrow bod

short, strong neck

three strong fingers
on each hand

short front legs

powerful back legs

The body of the Allosaurus was built for hunting. It walked on two back legs which were very strong and which helped it to run fast. Some scientists think the Allosaurus could run as fast as a person.

However, the Allosaurus would have fallen flat on its face if it hadn't been for its long, thick tail. The tail balanced the body of the Allosaurus as it ran.

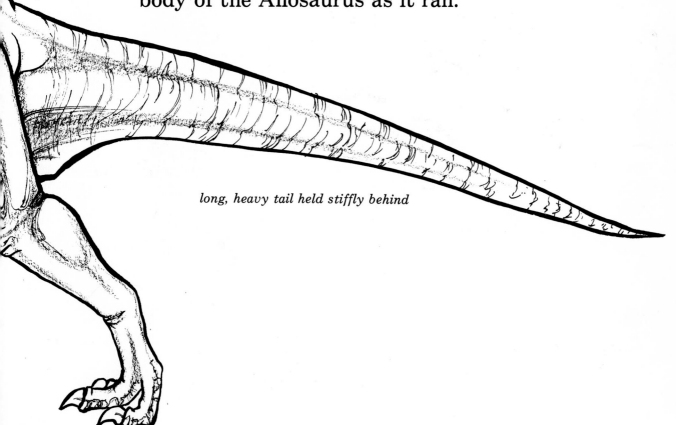

long, heavy tail held stiffly behind

birdlike feet with three claws

The Allosaurus' two front arms were very short, but each one had three sharp claws to rip apart meat.

The Allosaurus had bad table manners, though. It gulped its food down without even chewing. Its jaws were hinged so that they could open wide enough to swallow a small animal whole!

The Allosaurus hunted any animal it
wanted—the Stegosaurus, the Campto-
saurus, even the huge Apatosaurus and
Diplodocus.

You wouldn't think a creature who could hunt those dinosaurs would ever be afraid of anything.

But there was one thing that could stop
an Allosaurus . . .

deep water. The Allosaurus was afraid to
go into deep water, because it might get
stuck in the mud and not be able to get
out again.

Other dinosaurs were afraid of the Allosaurus, but Allosaurs liked each other. They lived and traveled in small herds. Together, they roamed the high, dry ground, going down into the swampy areas to hunt plant-eating dinosaurs.

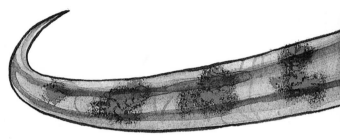

When Allosaurus babies hatched, scientists think that one or more adults protected and cared for them.

The adults brought the babies food and kept them safe from other kinds of dinosaurs. The other kinds thought baby Allosaurs made a great snack.

The babies, which were less than two feet long when born, needed to be cared for until they grew up—then the rest of the world had to watch out!

The Allosaurs all died many years ago, just as all the other dinosaurs did. No one knows for sure why.

Some scientists think a huge rock from space, called an asteroid, hit the earth. This could have changed the earth's temperature, causing the dinosaurs to freeze. Others think radiation from an exploding star may have killed the dinosaurs.

We will probably never know exactly what killed them, but it's nice to think that dinosaurs still live on in books, in movies, and in your imagination.

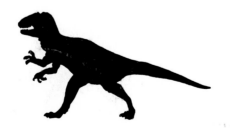